Guelph Pub.

TOOLS FOR CAREGIVERS

- **F&P LEVEL:** C
- **WORD COUNT:** 35

- **CURRICULUM CONNECTIONS:** nature, seeds, fruit, flowers

Skills to Teach

- **HIGH-FREQUENCY WORDS:** are, the, them, these, they, we
- **CONTENT WORDS:** flowers, fruit, green, grow(s), leaves, orange, pick, plant(s), red, seeds, tomato(es), turn, yellow
- **PUNCTUATION:** exclamation points, periods
- **WORD STUDY:** long /e/, spelled *ea* (*leaves*); long /e/, spelled *ee* (*green*, *seeds*); long /o/, spelled *ow* (*grow*, *yellow*); /oo/, spelled *ui* (*fruit*); /ow/, spelled *ow* (*flowers*)
- **TEXT TYPE:** information report

Before Reading Activities

- Read the title and give a simple statement of the main idea.
- Have students "walk" through the book and talk about what they see in the pictures.
- Introduce new vocabulary by having students predict the first letter and locate the word in the text.
- Discuss any unfamiliar concepts that are in the text.

After Reading Activities

Explain to readers that tomatoes are technically fruits. This is because they grow from a flower and have seeds. What other fruits can readers name? What do their seeds look like? How do those fruit seeds compare to tomato seeds?

Tadpole Books are published by Jump!, 5357 Penn Avenue South, Minneapolis, MN 55419, www.jumplibrary.com

Copyright ©2023 Jump. International copyright reserved in all countries. No part of this book may be reproduced in any form without written permission from the publisher.

Editor: Jenna Gleisner **Designer:** Molly Ballanger

Photo Credits: DustyPixel/iStock, cover; Madlen/Shutterstock, 1; Shutterstock, 2bl, 3; FotoDuets/Shutterstock, 4–5; fotografermen/Shutterstock, 2ml, 2mr, 6–7; Aviavlad/Shutterstock, 2tl, 8–9; gavran333/iStock, 2tr, 10–11; Another77/Shutterstock, 2br, 12–13; Ariel Skelley/Getty, 14–15; Studio 888/Shutterstock, 16.

Library of Congress Cataloging-in-Publication Data
Names: Sterling, Charlie W., author.
Title: Tomato / by Charlie W. Sterling.
Description: Minneapolis, MN: Jump!, Inc., (2023)
Series: See a plant grow! | Includes index. | Audience: Ages 3–6
Identifiers: LCCN 2021047467 (print) | LCCN 2021047468 (ebook)
ISBN 9781636907086 (hardcover)
ISBN 9781636907093 (paperback)
ISBN 9781636907109 (ebook)
Subjects: LCSH: Tomatoes—Life cycles—Juvenile literature.
Classification: LCC SB349 .S74 2023 (print) | LCC SB349 (ebook) | DDC 635/.642—dc23
LC record available at https://lccn.loc.gov/2021047467
LC ebook record available at https://lccn.loc.gov/2021047468

TOMATO

by Charlie W. Sterling

TABLE OF CONTENTS

tadpole
books

WORDS TO KNOW

flowers

fruit

leaves

plants

seeds

tomatoes

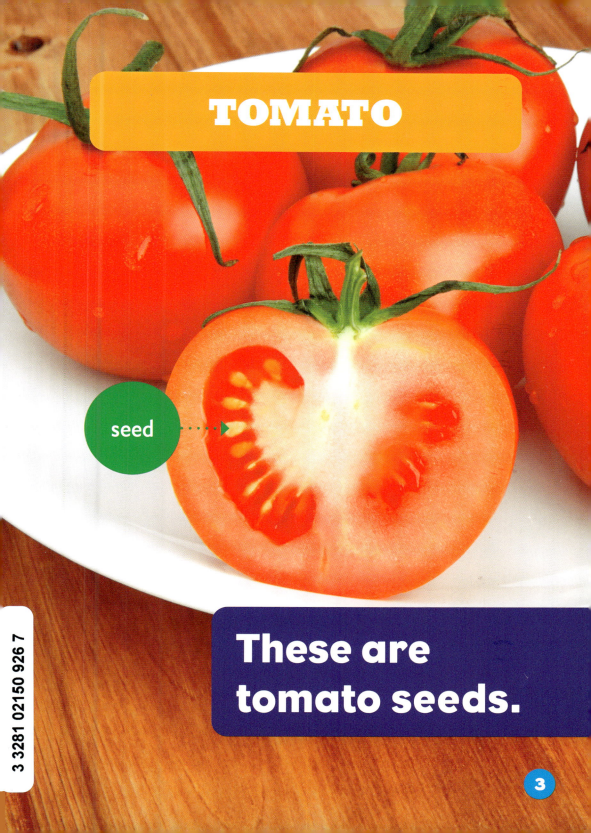

TOMATO

seed

These are tomato seeds.

seed

We plant them.

Green plants grow.

leaf

They grow leaves.

flower

They grow flowers.

They are yellow.

Fruit grows!

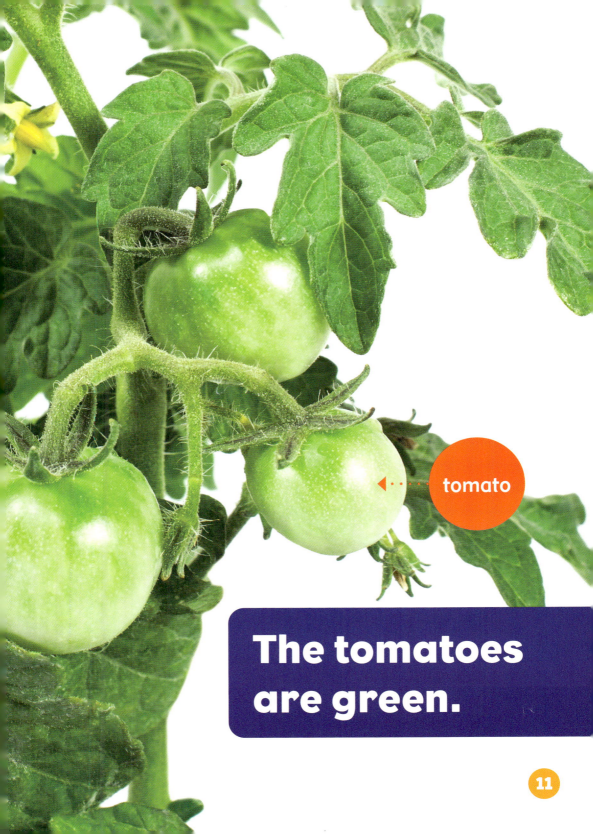

tomato

The tomatoes are green.

They turn orange.

They turn red.

14

We pick them!

LET'S REVIEW!

Tomatoes change color as they grow and ripen. What color is this tomato?

INDEX